JOHN RUTTER
ELEGY AND FESTIVE BELLS

MUSIC DEPARTMENT

OXFORD
UNIVERSITY PRESS

for Ian McMillan

1. Elegy

JOHN RUTTER

OXFORD UNIVERSITY PRESS MUSIC DEPARTMENT, GREAT CLARENDON STREET, OXFORD OX2 6DP
The Moral Rights of the Composer have been asserted. Photocopying this copyright material is ILLEGAL.

2. Festive Bells

JOHN RUTTER